RHYTHM OF THE EARTH

A TRIBUTE TO OUR PLANET

CHETANA HEGDE

Dedication

This book is dedicated to our planet—our first home and our greatest teacher. May these poems serve as a humble tribute to the beauty, resilience, and quiet wisdom of the Earth. And to all those who feel its rhythm in their hearts, may you continue to listen, protect and celebrate the wonder that surrounds us every day.

To my husband—my unwavering source of love and support. Your steady presence and constant encouragement gave me the courage to shape these thoughts into poetry.

To my son—your innocent questions, boundless curiosity, and wide-eyed wonder about the world reminded me why this Earth is so worth writing for. You helped me see nature through fresh eyes, and for that, I am endlessly grateful.

With deepest gratitude and love, this book is dedicated to my family and friends. Thank you for everything.

Contents

Contents

Preface

Dear Reader,

Welcome to **Rhythm of The Earth,** a collection of poems that celebrate the beauty, wonder, and wisdom of our planet. As a Geography teacher, I have always been fascinated by the beauty, complexity and story of our planet. Teaching about Earth's landforms, climates, and systems deepened my appreciation for the natural world and sparked a sense of wonder that goes beyond maps and facts. This wonder inspired me to express my thoughts not just through lessons, but through poetry.

Reading about Earth in a textbook is a common experience—a series of facts, figures, and explanations laid out in neat rows. But when we take a step beyond the ordinary, when we look at the Earth through the lens of poetry, we uncover a unique world where science and art meet. The shapes of mountains, the flow of rivers, the breath of the wind—these are not just phenomena to be studied, but stories to be told, emotions to be felt.   This book is a reflection of my admiration for the planet we call home—a way to honour its journey, its grace, and its quiet strength.

In this book, I aim to offer something different. While textbooks teach us the mechanics of Earth, poetry invites us to feel it, to experience its beauty, power, and mystery in a way that is both intellectual and emotional. Here, the Earth is not merely a subject to be understood, but a living, breathing entity to be embraced with wonder. Each poem seeks to capture the essence of Earth's grandeur, from the quiet hum of the soil to the vastness of the sky.

Rhythm of the Earth is born from deep admiration for our planet and growing concern for its future. Each piece is a reflection of wonder, grief, gratitude and hope. It is not just a tribute, but a call: to pause, to notice, and to reconnect.

To write about Earth in a poetic way is to celebrate its complexities in a form that touches the heart, rather than just the mind. It is a reminder that the world around us is not just a collection of facts—it is a poem, unfolding with every sunrise, every storm, every whisper of the wind.

This book is an attempt to bring together the answers to many of the questions that my students have asked over the years. It is a journey into the heart of Earth—exploring its history, its processes, and its place in the vast universe. I hope it not only satisfies their curiosity but also sparks a deeper appreciation and a lifelong interest in the world around us.

Yours,
Chetana Hegde

Acknowledgements

Writing Rhythm of the Earth has been a journey filled with learning, love, and inspiration. I would like to thank all my students, who have been a constant source of motivation. Your curiosity and enthusiasm for geography inspired me to explore new ways of sharing knowledge.

A special thanks to my family and friends for their endless support, encouragement, and belief in my dream. Your kind words and patience gave me the strength to keep writing.

I also want to thank my fellow teachers and mentors, who showed me the beauty of teaching and helped shape my path as an educator. And finally, to the Earth — the greatest teacher of all — thank you for your rhythm, your silence, and your song.

Yours,
Chetana Hegde

1. Birth of The Earth - A Cosmic Miracle

In the vast expanse of space and time,
A tiny blue dot, our Earth does shine.
A delicate balance of gravity and spin,
A cosmic miracle, where life can begin.

Eight planets revolving around the Sun's warm light,
Our Earth - a jewel in the dark of night.
In the dark of space, a light did shine,
A cosmic miracle born of dust and divine.

In ancient times, when fire did reign,
The Earth was born from volcanic pain.

Molten lava flowing like a sea.
A cosmic miracle where new life did release,

The Earth cooled down as ages passed,
And from the fire, a new world was cast.
Within the Milky Way's swirling curve,
Earth - A cosmic miracle is a tiny reserve.

From empty space, so still and bare,
Our Earth was born with love and care.
And ever since that wondrous day,
Earth - A cosmic miracle spins in space, in her own way.

2. After Earth's First Breath

The Earth was born, so hot and bright,
With fire and smoke and splashing light.
It spun around, a ball of flame,
But slowly changed and got a name.

The rain drops fell; the sky turned blue,
The oceans formed, the rivers too.
The land grew hard, the air turned clear,
And the tiny life began to cheer.

Small things swam in quiet seas,
They danced along the ocean breeze.
They grew and changed in sea and air,
Little by little, everywhere.

Now Earth is home to all to see,
To mountains, clouds and every sea.
She is still alive, she still can grow,
A special world we have come to know.

3. Rise of Humans on Earth

Long ago, on the Earth so wide,
Before there were cities, before human pride.
Lived creatures who walked on four,
But something in them wished for more.

They stood up tall, looked at the sky,
Wondering how and wondering why.
They used their hands to hold and make,
To build, to hunt, to cook, to bake.

Their faces were broad, with heavy brow,
Hairy bodies from head to toe,
Long arms, strong legs and steady feet,
Built for walking through grass and heat.

They made sharp stones and learned to fight,
They found the warmth in firelight.
They painted the stories on the wall,
Of animals, hunts and life so small.

They didn't know what they would be,
But they were learning, wild and free.
Step by step, their minds grew strong,
They started to know what's right and wrong.

From jungle paths to open land,
They walked together hand in hand.
The journey had just begun for all,
When humans rose and learned to stand tall.

4. Beginning of Agriculture on Earth

Long ago on Earth was vast and wide,
Early humans wandered far with pride.
They hunted food and gathered grain,
And moved through sun, and wind, and rain.

But then one day a change began,
A clever thought in woman or man.
"What if seeds we sow and grow,
Instead of always on the go?"

They tilled the soil, they watched it rise,
Green shoots reached up to greet the skies.
From wild grass came golden wheat,
From tiny seeds, a world to eat.

They planted grains like wheat and rice,
With barley, millet, oh so nice.
Lentils, beans, and maize took root.
In fields where once they searched for fruit.

They raised the sheep, the goat, the cow,
To help with work, and give them chow.
They learned to care, to feed, to breed,
And found in animals all they need.

No longer just to roam and roam,
They built the first of many homes.
Villages rose, then cities too,
From farming, all this life grew new.

Earth was shaped by plough and hand,
By farmers working with the land.
A quiet change, so deep, so wide,
The seeds of history sown with pride.

From ancient times to modern day,
Farming feeds us, lights the way.
It gives us food, it gives us life,
It ends our hunger, eases strife.

5. Earth – The Silent Witness of the Great Civilizations

I've seen empires rise, and I've seen them fall,
Civilizations born, and some lose their all.
I felt the heat of fire and stone,
As they carved their names into my bone.

In Egypt, I watched as Nile began to flow,
And pharaohs rose in golden glow.
With pyramids that touched the sky,
They dreamed of life that would not die.

In Mesopotamia, by the Tigris' flow,
They wrote their stories, letting knowledge grow.
The ziggurats stood, proud and tall,
I watched them rise, I saw them fall.

In the Indus Valley, a culture so grand,
Harappans thrived, with advanced plans in hand.

Sophisticated cities, with planned design,
Mohenjo-Daro's ruins, a legacy divine.

In China's land, the Great Wall stretched,
I felt the weight as it was etched.
The Silk Road's passage, where traders would roam,
Ancient dynasties, like Qin and Han's home.

I have seen Greece's glory, where democracy was born,
Olympia's legacy, forever sworn.
Philosophers like Socrates, wisdom did impart,
Theatre and arts, a cultural heart.

Through countless ages, near and far,
I've watched their dreams like falling stars.
And though they're gone, their whispers stay,
Carried in my heart, they'll never stray.

For I am Earth, I hold their name,
A witness to their rise and flame.
Through every dawn and every dusk,
Their legacies live in me, in trust.

6. Sacred Earth – Sacred Names

Oh divine Earth -
In ancient Greece, **Gaia** was your name,
The goddess of Earth, with a sacred flame.
The Greeks worshipped you, with rituals and prayers,
A goddess of fertility, with abundant cares.

In Hindu scriptures, **Bhudevi** is your name,
The goddess of earth, with a loving claim.
You are a woman, with many arms so fine,
Holding lotus, a symbol of divine design.

In China's heart, **Hou Tu** is your name,
The goddess of earth, with divine fame.
You are the one who brings forth life,
We celebrate you, with each new birth.

In the land of Incas, **Pachamama** is your name,
The goddess of earth, you're honoured the same.
You ae the one who gives us food, with each new day,
A symbol of abundance, in every single way.

In Africa, **Asase Yaa** is your name,
The goddess of earth forever in our frame.
They dance and sing, with drums beating strong,
A tribute to the earth, where their ancestors belong.

In Egypt's sands, **Geb** is your name,
The God of earth, your spirits flame.
You are the protector, of pharaohs so grand,
You always stay strong, in this ancient land.

In the land of Japan **Izanami** is your name,
In their hearts, your name's etched in fame.
You are the ray of hope, of new rebirth,
A symbol of wonder, on this earthly earth.

The earth is our mother, our guiding light,
A source of life, in the dark of night.
We must honour her, with every step we take,
And preserve her beauty, for our children's sake.

7. From Earth to Sky: The Scholars' Journey

Long ago, with eyes so keen,

Scholars looked at Earth unseen.

They wondered how the mountains rise,

And why the waves begin to rise.

Aristotle, a Greek scholar, was wise and bold,

Taught that Earth was truly round.

He watched the Earth with thoughtful eyes,

And questioned what lay in the skies.

Alfred Wegener, a German scholar had a plan,

He spoke of continents once a clan.

Drifting apart across the seas,

He proposed a theory known as "continental drift".

James Hutton, a Scottish scholar, saw the Earth's true face,

He spoke of time, a slow, vast race.

"The Earth is old," he boldly said,

And showed that rocks were born and dead.

Aryabhata, an Indian scholar, wise and bright,
Knew Earth spun in day and night.
And when India's dreams reached for the sky,
The first satellite soared so high.
Aryabhata was its name,
A symbol of India's space-born fame.

Varahamihira studied the sky,
He watched the stars and asked, "Why?"
He saw the Earth's place in the stars,
A world in space, a planet far.

Dr. Vikram Sarabhai, had a great vision,
Laid the foundation for India's space mission.
His dreams reached the stars, beyond the sky,
And in his path, India learned to fly.

Marie Tharp, an American Geologist, mapped ocean's floor,
Her maps revealed much to explore.
With lines of depth, she showed the way,
To understand the world's ocean sway.

From **Darwin's** theory of evolution's might,
To **Einstein's** theory of bending of light.
The great minds from East to West,
Each one in search of Nature's quest.

They've walked the Earth, both far and wide,
Their wisdom spread from side to side.
Each one left marks upon the land,

Guiding us with knowledge grand.

8. Earth's Inner World – Layer by Layer

Deep below the ground, lies a world unseen
Layers of earth, in silence serene
Where heat and pressure twist and flow
There secrets of the planet grow.

The **Crust**, a shell, so thin and strong,
Where continents and oceans belong.
The surface layer, where we reside,
Home to mountains, valleys wide.

The Mantle comes next, thick and wide,
With melted rock that flows inside.
Known as Magma - It's hot and full of might,
It makes the crust move left and right!

The Core is centre, deep and round,
Where iron and nickel, both metals are found.
The outer core spins in liquid flow,
While solid inner core, burns deep below.

So now you know what lies below,
In Earth's great layers, down they go.
A world inside, so deep and grand,
Beneath our feet and all the land!

9. Tectonic Plates – The Secret Movers Below

Deep down below the land we know,
The Earth's big plates move kind of slow.
They float on melted rock so hot,
And shape the world, a lot, a lot!

The plates are giant puzzle pieces,
They move around in bits and pieces.
Though we can't see them move around,
They're always shifting underground.

They crash and push, or slide away,
And change the Earth a bit each day.
They build up mountains, tall and wide,
Or make deep oceans, side by side.

Sometimes they shake, and that's a quake,
The ground will rumble, jump, and break.
Sometimes a volcano might blow,
With lava flowing fast and slow.

So next time when you feel the ground,
Just think of plates that move around.
They shape the Earth in many ways,
And have been moving for all days!

10. Gravity: Earth's Quiet Grip

There's a force we do not see,
But it holds all – even land and sea.
It keeps our feet upon the ground,
And makes the planets go around.

It pulls the rain, it drops the ball,
It keeps the rivers from a fall.
It holds the moon, it lifts the tide,
It keeps the stars in place outside.

This force is called **gravity,**
A gift from Earth to you and me.
It hugs us tight, both big and small,
So we don't float or drift at all.

Without its pull, we would fly away,
Like feathers in a breeze each day.
But thanks to gravity so strong.
We walk, we run, we dance along.

It's quiet, calm, and always near,
A force that works both far and clear.
So thank you, Earth, for holding tight,
For keeping us in place just right.

11. Earth's Air Blanket – The Layers Above

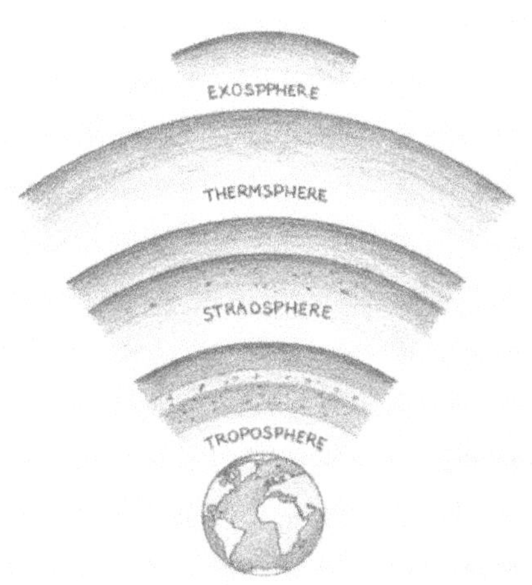

Many planets have air so thin or thick,
With gases that can make you sick.
But Earth's the one with air just right,
To breathe, to live, from day to night.

Above the hills, beyond the sea,
A veil surrounds both you and me.
Invisible, yet always near,
The breath of life, the Atmosphere.

The **troposphere** is down below,
Where winds do blow and raindrops go.
It's where we live and breathe and play,
With clouds and weather every day.

Above it sits the **stratosphere,**
With jets that zoom and skies so clear.
This is the layer where silence grows,
And ozone guards us from sun's blows.

The **mesosphere** is cold and high,
Where shooting stars burn in the sky.
Though no one lives up in this space,
It keeps rocks from the human race.

Then comes the **thermosphere** so wide,
Where auroras shimmer, side to side.
The space station floats in this zone,
So far from Earth, yet not alone.

The last is called the **exosphere,**
Where air is thin and satellites soar.
It slowly fades to outer space,
The final edge of Earth's embrace.

So, five great layers guard our Sphere,
Together called the **atmosphere**!

12. The Blue Planet : The Only One With Water and Life

In the universe so huge and infinite,
Only Earth has life and water in it.

It shines with water, fresh and clear,
The only one with oceans near.
No other planet has such seas,
With dancing waves and swaying trees.

The sun warms seas, the water flies,
It forms white clouds up in the skies.
Then rain comes down to land once more,
To streams and lakes and ocean shore.

The water cycle spins around,
From sky to land, then underground.
It rains, it flows, then climbs up high,
To form new clouds across the sky.

From snowy hills to sandy shore,
Water flows forever more.
It gives us life, it helps us grow,
It cools the sun and melts the snow.

That's why we call her the "Blue Planet,"
With lakes and oceans like a blanket.
Protect her skies, protect her blue,
She gives us life in all we do.

13. Four Domains – Together They Make Earth

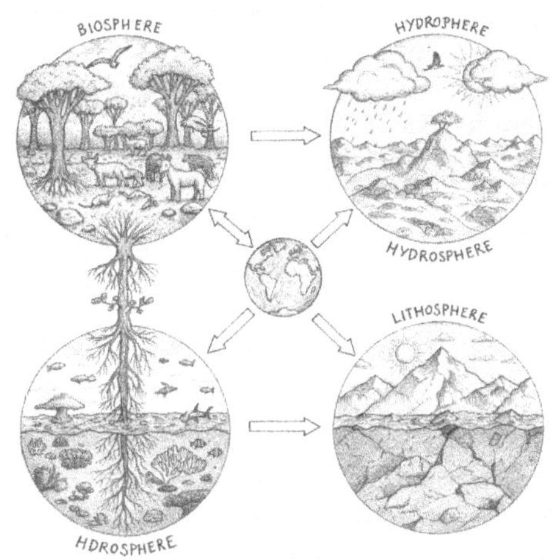

Our Earth is made of four great parts,
Each one with roles and special arts.
Land, water, air, and life so dear,
Together they make our world so clear!

The **land** is called the **lithosphere,**
With hills and rocks and ground so near.
Mountains tall and valleys low,
It's where we walk and plants can grow.

The water part is **hydrosphere,**
With lakes and seas both far and near.
Rain and rivers, ice and snow,

Water helps all life to grow.

The air around is **atmosphere,**
It gives us wind and skies so clear.
We breathe it in, so wild and free,
It holds the clouds and birds so free.

The **biosphere** is full of life,
With trees and bees and birds in flight.
People, animals, plants and more,
Life lives here and so much more.

These four domains work hand in hand,
To shape the sea, the sky, the land.
Each one plays a perfect role,
Together they make our planet whole.

14. Earth's Polar Extremes

At the top and bottom ends,
Where Earth begins and gently bends.
There lie the poles, so cold and wide,
With ice and snow on every side.

The North and South, where cold winds blow,
Covered deep in ice and snow.
The Arctic's icy seas, the Antarctic's snowy peak,
Two extremes of nature, in a delicate seek.

The North Pole floats on ocean deep,
Where polar bears and white seals sleep.
The sun stays up for days in June,
Then disappears beneath the moon.

The South Pole stands on land so high,
Where penguins walk and cold winds fly.
The ice is thick, the air is dry,
And stars shine bright in the dark sky.

The poles, though distant, both cold and bold,
Are part of the balance the Earth must hold.
They regulate the climate and the ocean's flow,
A vital feature that all must know.

15. Landscapes – Shaped by Nature's Hand

The Earth is shaped in many ways,
With hills and plains and ocean bays.
From mountain peaks that touch the sky,
To deserts where the winds blow dry.

The mountains tower, strong and high,
The oceans deep, with secret nigh.
The forests green, with ancient might,
The deserts, shine in the golden light.

Plateaus are high with flat, wide land,
While rolling hills by meadows stand.
Islands rest in oceans blue,
And valleys hide with peaceful view.

The creatures roam, in diverse throng,
From mighty beasts to tiny song.
The winds whisper, through the trees so tall,
The rivers flow with a gentle call.

Let us cherish, this gift so rare,
Let us protect, this planet we share.
Let us preserve, this beauty and might,
For future generations, a guiding light.

16. Mountains – Giants of Earth

Mountains tall and mountains high,
Touching the sky, they touch the eye.
Their peaks so sharp, their slopes so steep,
A challenge to climb, a wonder to keep.

Everest stands, the highest of all,
A frozen queen, so vast and tall.
In the Himalayas, cold and bright,
It shines with snow, so pure and white.

K2 is fierce, steep and wild,
Dangerous paths, few have smiled.
A mountain tough, where storms arise,
Challenging all who dare to rise.

Kilimanjaro, lone and high,
Touches Africa's open sky.

With golden plains that stretch so far,
It shines beneath the moon and stars.

The Alps stand proud with peaks so white,
A snowy charm, a skier's delight.
From France to Swiss and Austria's land,
They stretch with beauty, tall and grand.

The Rockies roll through west so wide,
With forests green and rivers beside.
A land of bears, of trails untold,
With sunsets painting peaks in gold.

Mountains rise, so bold, so grand,
Nature's wonders shape the land.
Standing strong through time and tide.
Forever proud, forever wide.

17. Mighty Oceans – Guardians of the Blue

The oceans vast, so deep, so wide,

Where waves and winds and wonders hide.

They touch the shores of every land,

With secrets buried in the sand.

The Pacific, so wide and deep,

The largest ocean has many secrets to keep.

Its waves can roar, its storms can rise,

Yet sunsets paint its endless skies.

The Atlantic, bold and strong,

With tides that sing an ancient song.

Ships have sailed from shore to shore,

Telling tales of days of yore.

The Indian Ocean, warm and bright,
Shines beneath the golden light,
It kisses lands with gentle waves,
And holds the paths where sailors brave,.

The **Southern Ocean**, cold and bold,
Circles Antarctica, icy and old,
Penguins play where the waters freeze,
Beneath the winds and snowy breeze.

The **Arctic Ocean**, small and shy,
Lives near the top, where polar bears lie,
Its icy heart beats soft and slow,
Where not too many people go.

The oceans wide, all five we see,
Moving with strength and mystery,
They keep us cool, they help us live,
So much to learn, and so much to give.

18. Deserts - Dry and Dazzling Places of Earth

Far and wide across the land,
Deserts stretch like golden sand.
Hot and dry, with skies so blue,
Let's explore a few with you!

The Sahara in Africa's heart,
Is the biggest desert to start.
Camels walk through dunes so high,
Underneath the blazing sky.

The Kalahari's vast and sandy ground,
A desert in Africa, where lions are found
Trees and grass grow here and there,
It's not all sand, there's life to spare!

The Gobi in Mongolia's land,
Has rocky ground, not just sand.
Cold at night and hot by day,
Yaks and foxes find their way.

Arabian Desert, dry and deep,
Where sandstorms swirl and camels' sleep.
With date palms growing near a stream,
It feels just like a desert dream.

The Atacama's dry and bare,
In South America, rain is rare!
Mountains watch the desert plain,
It might not see a drop of rain.

The Thar in India, bright and bold,
Has forts and tales from days of old.
The Aravalli hills, stand tall and strong,
Peacocks dance and camels' roam.

Deserts may be hot or cold,
With ancient secrets to unfold.
They may seem empty, dry, and bare,
But look around—life's everywhere!

19. Islands and Coastal – Whispers of the Shore

The islands rise, from the ocean's blue,
A haven for life, in a watery hue.
Their shores so fine, their sands so warm,
A tropical paradise, with natural charm.

Soft white sand, beneath bare feet,
Coconut scent, in every beat.
Ocean breeze, that whispers low,
A soothing melody, as waves flow.

The land and sea meet side by side,
Where waves come in and then they slide.
Some shores are rocky, sharp and high,
Some are flat beneath the sky.

The coastline's beauty, a treasure to see,
A place where the earth, meets the sea.
The waves' gentle lap, a soothing sound,
A calming presence, that's always around.

Each place has stories it can tell,
Of storms that came, or where boats fell.
From beaches wide to hidden bays,
They're changing slowly, day by day.

So let's enjoy each shore and isle,
Where sea and land can make you smile.
They're gifts from Earth, both big and small,
With so much beauty, one and all.

20. Rivers - Earth's Flowing Veins

The mighty rivers flow through the earth,
Shaping the world and giving us rebirth.
Source of wonder and source of life,
They flow with the force of strife.

The Nile River flows through Egypt's land,
Where giant and mysterious pyramids stand.
Built great structures, that touch the sky,
A river of wonder, where history meets the eye.

The Amazon River flows through Brazil's heart,
Where rainforests grow, and animals play their part.
Monkeys swing, and birds take flight,
A river of adventure, where nature shines so bright.

The Congo's mystery, a journey so dark,
Flows through Africa, where jungles embark.
A river of wonder, where wildlife thrives,
Where the heart of darkness, and adventure survives.

The Ganga's sacred waters, a spiritual sight,
Flows through India, where temples bless the land.
A river of faith, where pilgrims bath and pray,
Where the Himalayas, a majestic backdrop sway.

The Thames flows gently through London town,
Past bridges old and streets of renown.
It tells the tales of days gone by,
Beneath the misty English sky.

Let's cherish these rivers, and the world they share,
Keep them clean and healthy, for future generations to care.
They bring us joy, and wonder to see,
The rivers of the world, a gift for humanity.

21. A Forest for Every Place

Earth has forests, far and wide,
On mountains tall, by oceans' side.
Each one different, each one special,
Home to birds and trees so tall.

Rainforests are warm and green,
With leaves so thick, the sun's unseen.
Birds sing loud, and monkeys play,
In trees that stretch and sway all day.

Deciduous forests change each year,
Their leaves turn gold when cold is near

In spring they bloom, in fall they fall.
A lovely dance we all recall.

Tundra forests near the snow,
Where lichens and mosses grow.
It's cold and quiet all around,
With frozen sky and frozen ground.

Mountain forests climb so high,
They almost reach the clouds and sky.
The air is thin, the world feels new,
With pine trees, rocks, and mountain view.

Desert forests may seem dry,
But plants still grow and reach the sky.
With strong, thick skin and roots so deep,
They drink the drops the sky does weep.

Forests help the Earth to breathe,
With every branch and every leaf.
Let's care for them, both big and small,
They are the heart, the lungs of all.

22. The Continents Tale

Africa, Asia, Europe, and more,
Once joined together, on a distant shore.
A supercontinent, Pangaea was the name,
Where continents converged, like a game.

The continents drifted, slowly apart,
Over millions of years, a gradual start.
The tectonic plates, they shifted and moved,
Creating oceans, and mountains improved.

The Atlantic Ocean, a rift did form,
As Africa and South America began to storm.
The Indian subcontinent, a journey did take,
To collide with Asia, and the Himalayas make.

The continents continue, their slow move,
Shaping the Earth's surface, a constant groove.
The Earth's crust, it's broken and worn,
As the continents drift, their paths are reborn.

Today we see, the continents so grand,
Africa's savannas, to Asia's mountain land.
Europe's cities, to the Americas' shore,
Each continent unique, yet connected evermore.

From Asia's peaks to Australia's shore,
Through Europe's charm and Africa's roar.
North and South America stand tall,
And icy Antarctica amazes us all.

The continents' tale, a story so old,
Of movement and change, forever to be told.
A testament to, the Earth's dynamic might,
The continents drift, through day and night.

23. Stone Stories : The Journey of Rocks on Earth

Rocks on Earth are not the same,
They change their form, but stay in name.
Let me tell you, come along,
The rock cycle is like a song.

Igneous rocks are first in line,
They come from lava, hot and fine.
When lava cools, hard rocks appear,
Granite and **basalt** form right here!

Then wind and rain break rocks apart,
They turn to bits, a brand new start.
These bits get pressed in layers tight,
Sedimentary rocks come into sight.
Sandstone and **limestone** layered just right.

But deep inside the Earth so wide,
Rocks feel heat and squeeze inside.
They slowly change, they twist and glow,
Metamorphic rocks begin to grow,
Marble and **slate** with shiny glow.

And sometimes heat will rise again,
The rocks may melt just like back then.
They turn to magma, hot and bright,
And **igneous rocks** return to light.

Round and round the rocks do go,
Changing shapes so very slow.
This is Earth's own magic style
The rock cycle goes on a while!

The rock cycle keeps Earth fresh and new,
It builds the land and shapes the view.
It gives us soil, strong stones, and more,
A gift from Earth we should adore.

24. From Red to Black : Earth's Soil Story

The Earth has many kinds of land,
Different soils in every strand.
Each type helps the plants to grow,
In sunshine, rain, and winds that blow.

Red soil shines like rusted clay,
Found where the sun shines all day.
It's good for crops that need dry heat,
A strong, warm ground beneath your feet.

Black soil is soft and deep and wide,
With cotton fields on every side.
It holds the rain, it keeps things wet,
The best for farming you can get.

Laterite soil is hard and red,
In places where the rain has spread.
It cracks in sun, it feels so dry,
But still, some plants can live nearby.

Alluvial soil by rivers stays,
It comes with floods, then slowly lays.
It's full of life and rich and fine,
Where farmers plant in rows and line.

Desert soil is dry and bare,

With scorching sun and dusty air.

Though water's rare and shade is few,

Some life still finds a way to bloom through.

Peaty soil is dark and wet,

In swamps and bogs, the ground is set.

It holds old plants from long ago,

And helps new little green things grow.

So many soils beneath our feet,

Each one special, each one neat.

The Earth gives us this lovely ground,

Where life and roots and dreams are found.

25. Sun and the Earth - The Eternal Cosmic Bond

The Earth and Sun, a celestial pair,
Dancing through space, with gravity's care.
Their bond is ancient, forged in the cosmic fire,
A relationship that fuels life's desire.

The sun, a star, that shines so bright,
Illuminates the earth, with its radiant light.
Warming the oceans, and nourishing the land,
Giving life to all, that's held in its hand.

The Earth, a planet, that spins with gentle ease,
Receives the sun's energy, with a grateful breeze.
Their orbits twisted, in a delicate balance,
A harmony that's precise, in the universe's dance.

Their relationship is one, of give and take,
The sun gives light, the earth gives life to make.
A cosmic bond that was created in the past,
A divine connection, that will forever last.

26. In the Arms of the Sun

Dear Sun, I see you every day,
Rising up without delay.
You shine so bright, you light my skies,
And gently help my plants arise.

You warm my seas, you melt my snow,
You make the rivers sing and flow.
You help my trees grow big and tall,
And bring soft light when rainclouds fall.

Because of you, the flowers bloom,
They dance with joy, they chase the gloom.
The bees come buzzing, life begins,
With every ray, the world still spins.

My meadows smile in colours wide,
With daisies, roses side by side.
You paint my hills in golden light,
And turn my darkest hours bright.

You wake the birds; they sing so clear,
Their songs are ones I love to hear.
The forests hum, the oceans gleam,
Because of you, I live and dream.

You give and give, and never tire,
A ball of light, a heart of fire.

You never ask for rest or pay,
Yet still you come and light the way.

So here's my thanks, from land to sea,
For all you do, for loving me.
I'm Earth, your friend, your biggest fan,
Thank you, Sun—my golden man.

27. Moon – The Constant Companion

I, Earth, have a friend so dear,

The Moon, my constant companion, always near.

We dance together, in the cosmic sea,

The gravitational bond, never allows us to be free.

Oh Moon! my true companion,

Your silvery radiance, illuminates my night,

Your comforting presence, that chases away my fright.

Oh Moon! my best companion,

You are the reason for my oceans' tide,

From new to full, you wax and wane with a gentle pride.

Oh Moon! my faithful companion,
In your gentle light, the stars shine bright ,
A soothing balm, that calms the heart's delight.

Oh Moon! my glowing companion,
You've seen my mountains, seas, and skies,
Reflected dreams in countless eyes.

Oh Moon! my patient companion,
Though far above, you feel so near,
A friend who listens, always here.

Oh Moon! my real companion,
You are my friend and partner in the skies
I pray for our bond, that never dies.

28. Eclipse – When I Make a Shadow

I am the Earth, round and wide,
With the Moon and Sun by my side.
We play a game up in the sky,
Sometimes we block each other's light—oh my!

When I move between Sun and Moon,
The moon turns red, like a silent flame.
That's a **lunar eclipse**, so calm, so deep,
As the Moon hides in my shadow's sleep.

And when the Moon comes in the way,
Of the bright and shining Sun one day.
It blocks the light for a little while,
That's a **solar eclipse**, with a shadowy smile.

So, when the Sun or Moon grows dim,
Just know it's part of our lovely spin.

Next time shadows cross your view,
Know it's me—just passing through.

Some gaze in awe, some hide in fear,
Some bang drums when shadows near.
Legends rise with every shade,
As myths and meanings are handmade.
But whether wonder, prayer, or fright,
All feel the magic in that light.

29. To My Starry Friends

When the world is wrapped in night,
And oceans shine in silver light.
I lift my face toward skies so high,
To greet my starry friends across the sky.

They blink and shimmer far away,
But keep me company till day.
They saw me born, they've watched me grow,
They know my storms, my fire, my snow.

They whisper tales from long ago,
Of suns that died and still they glow.
They guide the ships, they light the skies,
They glitter in different groups and patterns,
You call them with different names.

When humans gaze with wondering eyes,
I smile, beneath those ancient skies.
For though I'm small, I feel their grace,
My glittering friends in endless space.
And humans sing from near and far,
"Twinkle, twinkle, little star..."

30. Earth and Her Skybound Kin

I am Earth, the pulsing globe,
Clothed in blue, alive, alone.
But not unloved. My skies are wide,
And kin drift close on every side.

Brother Asteroid grumbles by,
Scarred and rough, a stubborn guy.
"Just passing through," he likes to say,
"But once I brushed you, back one day".

Long ago, brother asteroid came to visit me,
It lit my skies with fire and flame.
The dinosaurs were swept away,
A silent end to their glorious day.

Sister Meteorite—such flair!
She dances through my evening air,
"I burn for you," she sighs, then dies.
A golden tear that marks my skies.

Old Uncle Comet, hooded in ice,
Returns with tales from Paradise.
He hums of stars I've never known,
And weeps a trail when heading home.

Halley comet comes with shining tail,
A glowing ghost through starry veil.
"I'll see you soon," she says, then flies,
For you it is once in a lifetime through my skies.

So, I am not alone, I never was,
I have relatives in the universe so vast.
They speak, they move, they breathe with me,
This is my grand celestial family.

31. Earth : In Motion, Always

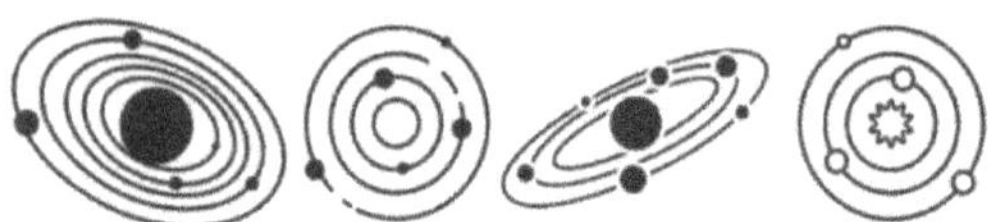

Have you ever wondered why day turns to night?
Or how seasons change from cold to bright?
It's all because Earth loves to move,
With two special steps in a graceful groove.

Earth's **rotation** is steady and true,
It spins around, the whole day through.
From morning light to evening's rest,
This spinning makes day and night.

Then comes the **revolution**, a journey so wide,
Around the Sun, Earth takes a ride.
It takes a year, through each new season,
Changing the weather, for every reason.

Rotation makes day, **revolution** brings the year,
A constant rhythm, both far and near.
Together they shape the world we see,
Giving life to all, as far as can be.

32. Earth's Daily Dance

When morning comes, I slowly wake,
The stars fade out, the skies turn pale.
The Sun peeks up, so soft and bright,
And gently fills my face with light.

He climbs up high and warms my skin,
Lights up the trees, the seas, the wind.
The clouds glow gold, the sky turns blue,
A brand new day begins, feels new.

The world is alive, and creatures roam,
Their footsteps quiet, in the morning's home.
The day goes on, and then it fades,
As sunset approaches, with its gentle shades.

The colours change, and night falls slow,
A peaceful evening, with a gentle glow.
The stars come out, like diamonds bright,
A beautiful night, with a calming sight.

I've seen this cycle, day after day,
As the sun rises, and sets in its way.
A never-ending dance, of morning and night,
A beautiful rhythm, that's always in sight.

33. Earth's Circle of Seasons

Earth wears her moods in seasons—vibrant in spring, fiery in fall, soft in snow, and golden in summer

The Earth keeps turning, round and round,
With seasons changing all year round.
Each one special, in its way,
A gift of nature, day by day.

Spring comes first with flowers bright,
The days grow warm, and full of light.
Birds sing songs and trees turn green,
It's the prettiest time you've ever seen.

Summer follows with sunny rays,
Nights are short with longer days.

Ice cream melts and beaches call,
It's the hottest time of all.

Then comes the **Rainy season** loud,
With thunder, lightning, and dark clouds.
The smell of wet earth fills the air,
A refreshing scent beyond compare.

Autumn comes with cooler air,
Leaves fall down everywhere.
Leaves turn gold, then red and brown,
Gently drifting to the ground.

Winter comes with snow so white,
The days are short, and long the night.
Footprints mark the morning snow,
As chilly winds begin to blow.

Each season brings its special way,
To colour life and shape each day.
From bloom to sun, from rain to snow,
The Earth puts on a lovely show.
A circle drawn by time and grace,
Nature's dance, in every place.

34. Earth's Joy in the Rain

The earthy aroma after rain is the planet's perfume

The sky turns soft, the winds grow light,
The clouds roll in, a lovely sight.
I close my eyes and feel the breeze,
A rainy day is here to please.

The raindrops fall, a gentle song,
I've waited for this all year long.
They soak my soil, they feed my trees,
They fill the rivers, lakes, and seas.

With every drop, I feel so new,
The grass grows tall, the flowers too.
The crops arise in fields so wide,
The rain gives food and life with pride.

The farmers smile, the forests sing,
The frogs jump high, the songbirds wing.
The air is clean, the dust is gone,
The rainy season brings new charm.

Then comes the sun, just like a friend,
To paint the sky where raindrops end.
And there it is—so bright, so bold,
A rainbow made of dreams and gold.

Its colours glow—so rich, so high,
A gentle arc across the sky.
The children point with laughing eyes,
And cheer beneath the painted skies.

It arcs above with colours true,
A gift of light in red to blue.
It's like a hug across the sky,
A sign that joy is standing by.

So, when it rains, don't feel dismay,
The Earth is happy on that day.
The rain brings life, and makes things grow,
And rainbow displays nature's brightest show.

35. Hot, Mild and Cold : Earth's Climatic Zones

The Earth is a world with climates so wide,
From the scorching heat to the freezing tide.
Three zones divide the warmth and cold,
Each with a story to be told.

The Tropics receive the sun's bright ray,
With warmth and light both night and day.
Here it's hot, the skies are clear,
And summer's warmth is always near.

The Temperate Zone is mild and fair,
With warm summers and cool winters in the air.
Spring and fall bring gentle change,
With sunny days and temperatures strange.

The Polar zones are cold, with ice and snow,
Where the sun is low and winds do blow.
It's frosty and freezing, all year long,
A land where cold and snow belong.

36. Grids of the Globe : Woven by Latitude, Stitched by Longitude

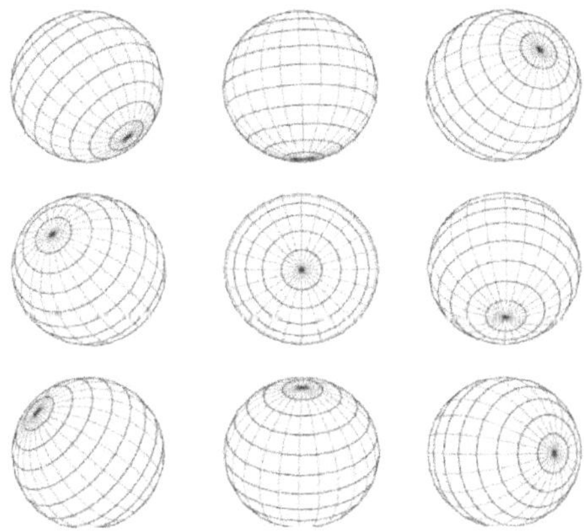

Invisible lines across the sphere,
Guiding sailors far and near.
One goes horizontal, the other vertical,
Together, they locate the places all.

Latitude belts the Earth like rings,
From Arctic chills to tropic springs.
Parallel bands from pole to pole,
Each one plays a vital role.

From zero at the equator's grace,
To ninety at each frozen place.
They tell us where the sun will shine,
In tropics warm or polar spine.

Longitude runs from top to base,
Through every time and every place.
Meridians meet at poles so tight,
But stretch apart in day and night.

The Prime Meridian, numbered nought,
Through Greenwich town, its path is caught.
To east or west, the numbers grow,
And time zones shift as longitudes flow.

Together, they make a mighty grid,
Revealing places once long hid.
A map's own soul, a navigator's song,
To tell us where we do belong.

So next you gaze at Earth so wide,
Think of the lines that gently guide.
Not seen, but felt in every chart,
The frame of maps, the globe's true heart.

37. Chasing the Sun: A Journey Through Solstices

The Earth goes round the mighty Sun,
A quiet trip that's never done.
And as we go, the seasons show,
With light and dark in gentle flow.

Summer Solstice, longest day,
The Sun is high, bright all the way.
June 21st, the time it stays,
With warmer nights and sunny days.

Winter Solstice, cold and deep,
The Sun is low, it seems to sleep.
December's days are short and shy,
The moon comes early to the sky.

Spring Equinox brings equal light,
Day and night in balance right.
March wakes flowers, birds take wing,
The Earth feels fresh with signs of spring.

Autumn Equinox comes with gold,
Leaves fall down as winds grow cold.
Day and night again the same,
Till winter comes to play its game.

So every year, this dance goes on,
With changing light from dusk to dawn.
A solar rhythm, slow and true,
The Sun and Earth in steps they knew.

38. The Wonders I Hold

I am the Earth, so strong and wide,
With secrets in my rocky hide.
I hold the wonders time has made
In light and shadow, sun and shade.

My **valleys** rest between the hills,
With flowers, trees, streams that thrill.
They're quiet, calm, and full of green,
A peaceful place, a lovely scene.

My **waterfalls** come rushing down,
From rocky cliffs, they splash and sound.
They sparkle bright and fall so free,

Like silver dancing just for me.

I carve **canyons**, deep and wide,
Rivers flow there with equal pride.
Waterfalls cascade, in misty veil,
A symphony, that echoes through my vale.

My **forests** so dense, wild and green,
A breathing world, a living scene.
Each root and rock, each bird and tree,
A precious part of what makes me.

All these gifts I give with care,
To all who live and breathe my air.
So love me well, and keep me clean,
Protect my lands and keep them green.

39. Gifts of the Earth

The Earth is kind, the Earth is wise,
It gives us life beneath the skies.,
With roots below and skies above
It wraps the world in endless love.

It gives us **trees** with branches wide,
To shade us from the sun outside.
Their leaves so green, their trunks so strong,
They release the oxygen, all day long.

It gives us **fruits**, so sweet and bright,
Mangoes, apples delicious and ripe,
Bananas, berries, juicy pears,

Grown with care by Earth's own prayers.

It gives us **flowers**, soft and fair,
With petals bright and scented air.
Roses, lilies, daisies too,
In every shade of every hue.

It gives us **grains** and golden wheat,
So, every soul has food to eat.
From rice fields wide to corn so tall,
The Earth provides enough for all.

Let's care for Earth with gentle hands,
For all it gives, both big and small,
The Earth's the greatest gift of all.

40. Earth's Hidden Wealth - Treasure in the Depth

Deep inside the Earth below,
Lie treasures formed so long ago.
Coal so black and oil so thick,
Made from plants and stone so quick.

Minerals sparkle, metals shine,
Copper, gold, and silver fine.
Diamonds hiding out of sight,
Sleeping in the darkest night.

Fossil fuels from ancient days,
Power cities, light our ways.

Oil and gas from long ago,
Help the cars and engines go.

The Earth gives soil, rich and deep,
Where seeds can grow and roots can sleep.
From tiny seeds to fields so wide,
It grows our food with quiet pride.

From mountain top to ocean floor,
The Earth provides us more and more.

But we must use them with great care,
So, all these gifts are always there.
Share the Earth and let it grow,
For future ones we'll never know.

41. What Have We Done to Earth?

The Earth was green, the skies were blue,
The flowers bloomed; the rivers flew.
But now we see a different face,
A fading world, a hurting place.

We build our towers, tall and wide,
But leave the trees to fall and die.
We fill the skies with smoke and flame,
Then wonder why the storms became.

The rivers once ran pure and clear,
Now choke on waste we toss each year.
The ocean's full of plastic waste,
The winds now blow with bitter taste.

We dig, we burn, we take, we throw,
Ignoring what the Earth must show.
We call it progress, loud and proud,
But silence falls beneath the cloud.

The creatures suffer, their numbers fall,
And still, we build our concrete wall.
We call it growth, we chase the speed,
But lose the things we truly need.

The earth gives us, its precious wealth,
We repay with, toxic health.
Let's stop the harm, let's heal the earth,
For our own sake, give nature rebirth.

42. A Warming World, A Weeping Earth

The forest stood, so green, so grand,
With birds and beasts that roamed the land.
The trees would dance, the winds would sing,
And nature felt like everything.

But slowly came the axe and flame,
And trees fell down, not one remained.
To build more roads, to make more space,
We took the forest's peaceful place.

The air grew warm, the rains grew thin,

The Earth began to change within.
The ice caps melt, the oceans rise,
The smoke and heat fill up the skies.

We call this change "global warming",
The Earth is sending us a warning.
Hotter days and stronger storms,
Are signs of new and dangerous forms.

The animals now have no home,
The soil is dry, the rivers roam.
The balance lost, the Earth feels weak,
She cries in storms, in floods that speak.

But if we plant and care once more,
And guard the trees we had before,
The Earth can heal, the skies can clear,
And nature's song we'll always hear.

43. Junk in My Space : Too Much to Carry

We reached for the stars, but forgot to clean up after ourselves

I spin in silence, blue and round,
With skies so vast and oceans sound.
But now I feel a heavy weight,
Not from within, but outer gate.

Once stars alone would dance with me,
Now metal floats where none should be.
Satellites hum in crowded rings,
And space is full of broken things.

You sent them up to learn, to spy,

To talk across the open sky.
But left behind without a care,
Scraps of steel are just floating there.

My night no longer calm and deep,
Your space machines disturb my sleep.
I try to breathe, to hold my grace,
But feel the clutter crowding space.

Please clean the mess you've made so high,
Don't fill my arms, or choke my sky.
I gave you ground, I gave you air,
Treat my space with equal care.

44. A Green Planet, in a Grey War

I Earth, was once a peaceful place,
With green trees and a smiling face.
The sky was blue, the air was clean,
The world was calm, the world was green.

But now there's war in every land,
With fire, smoke, and broken sand.
I feel sad, my heart is sore,
I don't smile like before.

My rivers bleed, my forests burn,
I wait for peace to return.
My mountains shake, my flowers fade,
I am tired of the mess you have made.

I watched you grow, I saw your dreams,
I gave you rivers, lakes, and streams.
But now I see the skies turn grey,
With bombs and smoke, day after day.

"O humankind," I now plead,
"Lay down your guns, leave your greed.
Care for me, and care for each other,
Every person is your sister or brother."

Why must you fight? Why must you hate?
You still have time—it's not too late.
Hold hands, not guns; speak words, not fear,
Bring back the peace I hold so dear.

45. Extinctions, Pandemics and the Planet

Through storms, through fire, through ancient fears,
She felt the weight of wars and loss.
Of stars that fell and rivers' cost.

Long ago, life first began,
But soon came warnings, part of the plan.
For every plant and creature bright,
A shadow hid, ready to fight.

The giants fell, the forests died,
In silence deep, with no one to guide.
Five times she watched the world go cold,

As nature's wrath took hold.

The dinosaurs vanished in a flash,
An asteroid's impact, an instant crash.
The Permian wiped out life's bloom,
As heat and toxins sealed their doom.

Then came the plagues, a bitter air,
The Spanish Flu, a world in despair.
The Black Death spread, so fierce and wild,
In its wake, the Earth beguiled.

Smallpox ravaged, and cholera too,
The world stood still, as death it drew.
Swine Flu spread with silent pace,
And Bird Flu followed, a deadly race.

Ebola came with fear and dread,
As many suffered, many fled.
And later, Corona's cruel spread,
A global grief, as fear was fed.

But some, too, were shaped by human hand,
From lab to market, across the land.
Through careless acts or silent trade,
Deadly paths for germs were laid.

When sickness spread and air turned bad,
People suffered, all were sad.
The Earth watched on with quiet grace,
Her wounds were deep, but not a trace.

So let us learn from her past pain,
The losses, grief, the endless rain.
For Earth remembers, Earth will mend,
And through it all, she'll still ascend.

46. When Earth Gets Angry

When Earth gets angry, she trembles and roars,
Shaking her mountains, cracking her floors.
She wakes the ground from quiet sleep
With quakes so strong, they shake the deep.

Her fiery heart begins to rise,
Volcanoes burst beneath the skies.
A molten scream, a lava flow,
A warning in her molten glow.

Deep in the sea, where silence lies,
She stirs the seas with mighty hands.
Tsunami crashes on the land,
With roaring waves and sweeping sand.

She loosens hills that once stood tall,
And sends down rocks in deadly fall.
A landslide tumbles with a cry,
Dust and boulders flying high.

Each natural disaster, a voice, a plea,
"Take care of nature, care for me."
For Earth may rumble, crash, and burn,
But peace is hers, if we return.

47. Bring Back Earth's Glory

Dear Earth, we know we've caused you grief,
Your forests cry, your days are brief.
But let us change, and try to be,
A friend to land, to sky, to sea.

Oh Earth, so patient, strong, and wise,
We see the pain behind your eyes.
It's not too late — we still can mend,
To treat you kindly, like a friend.

Let forests grow, let waters heal,
Let nature breathe, let balance feel.
For every seed and grain of sand,

Deserves a gentle, caring hand.

Let's plant a tree where none have grown,
And give the Earth a greener throne.
Let rivers dance and forests sing,
And watch the magic nature brings.

Let's clean the seas and clear the skies,
And wipe the tears from nature's eyes.
Reduce, Reuse, Recycle, we'll do our part,
Heal the earth, with a loving heart.

Ride a bike or walk a mile,
Let sunlight warm us with a smile,
Say no to plastic, loud and strong,
And teach the world what's right from wrong.

Protect the bees, the birds, the breeze,
Grow gardens full of fruits and trees.
With every act, both small and grand,
We heal the seas, the skies, the land.

Let's switch to green, energy so bright,
Use Solar and wind energy, time is right.
So let's begin, the time is now,
To take a step, to make a vow.
To love the Earth, restore her story,
And bring her back to all her glory.

48. Earth Day : A Global Call for Earth

Around the world, on Earth Day's call,
People rise together, one and all.
From distant shores to cities bright,
We join in harmony, taking flight.

In forests green, they plant a tree,
A seed of peace and purity.
On beaches wide, the clean-up crews,
Collect the trash, to start anew.

In towns and villages, children play,
Learning how to help Earth everyday.
Teachers share their hopeful voice,

For Earth's future, we must rejoice.

The winds that blow, the oceans wide,
Feel our love from every side.
From every land, from every place,
We honour Earth's gentle grace.

We march for forests, rivers, skies,
For oceans deep and stars that rise.
The world is calling, loud and clear,
To protect the Earth we hold so dear.

Leaders rise with thoughtful voice,
To guide the world, to make wise choice.
They speak of care, of greener ways,
And pledge their hearts to brighter days.

But when the speeches fade away,
And Earth Day turns to one more normal day.
Some promises float with the breeze,
Forgotten like the fallen leaves.

So, on this day, together we stand,
With open hearts and helping hands.
For Earth's our home, and we must care,
And Earth Day reminds us to be fair.

49. Future of the Earth

Dear Reader,

This page is yours! To dream, to wonder, to write. What do you see in Earth's tomorrow? A hope, a change, a shining light?

Pick up your pen, let your thoughts take flight... Happy writing.

50. Myths of the Earth

• 91 •

1. Hindu Mythology – Hiranya Garbha

In Hindu tradition, the universe originates from a golden cosmic egg or a golden cosmic womb known as *Hiranya Garbha*. From this egg, the first god, *Brahma*, emerges and creates the Earth and all living beings. This myth emphasizes the cyclical nature of creation and destruction in the universe.

2. Babylonian Myth – Enuma Elis

According to the Babylonian creation myth, *Enuma Elis*, the Earth was formed from the body of the primordial sea goddess *Tiamat*. After her defeat by the god *Marduk*, her body was divided to create the heavens and the Earth, illustrating the theme of order emerging from chaos.

3. Native American Myth – Earth Diver

Many Indigenous cultures in North America share the *Earth Diver* myth, where a waterfowl dives into the primordial ocean to bring up mud, which expands to form the Earth. This myth highlights the interconnectedness of all life and the sacredness of the Earth.

4. Chinese Myth - Pangu

In Chinese mythology, *Pangu* is a giant who emerges from a cosmic egg and separates the sky from the Earth. As he grows, his body transforms into various elements of the world: his breath becomes the wind, his voice thunder, his left eye the sun, his right eye the moon, and his body the mountains and rivers.

5. Greek Myth - Gaia

In Greek mythology, *Gaia* is the personification of the Earth. She is born from Chaos and gives birth to the sky, mountains, and sea. Gaia then produces the first gods and creatures, establishing her as the ancestral mother of all life.

6. Incan Myth - Viracocha

Inca mythology originated from Peru, specifically the Andean region where the Inca civilization flourished. The Inca civilization believed in *Viracocha*, the creator god who emerged from Lake Titicaca. He created the Earth, the sky, the sun, the moon, and all living beings. Viracocha then disappeared into the ocean, leaving behind a legacy of creation and divine order.

7. Yoruba Myth – Obatala and Olorun

Yoruba mythology originated from the Yoruba people, an ethnic group primarily located in southwestern Nigeria, as well as parts of Benin and Togo in West Africa. The region where they live is known as Yorubaland. In Yoruba mythology, the god *Obatala* descends from the sky on a golden chain with a snail shell filled with sand, a hen, and a black cat. He spreads the sand on the water, and the hen scratches it to form land. Obatala then plants a palm nut, which grows into a tree, and he creates humans from clay, breathing life into them with the help of *Olorun*, the supreme god.

8. Aztec Myth - Tlaltecuhtli

Aztec mythology originates from the Aztec civilization, which was centered in central Mexico. In Aztec mythology, the Earth goddess *Tlaltecuhtli* is dismembered by the gods *Quetzalcoatl* and *Tezcatlipoca*. Her body is divided, with the upper half becoming the sky and the lower half the Earth. Her features give rise to various natural elements: her skin becomes grasses and flowers, her hair trees and herbs, her eyes springs and wells, her nose hills and valleys, her shoulders mountains, and her mouth caves and rivers.

9. Norse Mythology – Ymir and the Creation

Norse mythology is the body of myths and beliefs originating from the North Germanic peoples, primarily from the Viking Age and earlier. After the gods defeated him, they used his body to shape the world: his flesh became the land, his blood formed the oceans, his bones turned into mountains, and his skull became the sky. From Ymir's eyebrows, they even created a place called **Midgard**, the home of humans.

10. Maori Mythology (New Zealand) – Rangi and Papa

Maori mythology comes from New Zealand, specifically from the indigenous Māori people. The Maori are a Polynesian people who have a rich oral tradition of myths and legends that explain the origins of the world and their connection to it. Sky Father (Rangi) and Earth Mother (Papa) were once tightly embraced, and their children lived in darkness between them. The gods pushed them apart to let light into the world.

These myths of the Earth speak to a time when the world was young in human memory, and every mountain, river, and star held a secret. These ancient tales, though shaped by imagination, reveal deep truths about our desire to understand and belong. As we walk the line between legend and knowledge, we find that myths are not just relics of the past, but timeless echoes of our curiosity and reverence for the planet we call home.

Though science has since offered new explanations, the myths remain—whispers of human wonder, imagination and our enduring connection to the Earth. They remind us that before we measured the planet, we dreamed it.